Really Useful P

What to say when you don't know what to say

edited by

Jonathan Romain

ISBN # 978-0-947884-20-8

This book is dedicated to the memory of Simon Franses
rabbi and colleague
1943-2009

First published in 2009 by
The Movement for Reform Judaism
The Sternberg Centre, 80 East End Road, London N3 2SY

www.reformjudaism.org.uk

Printed and bound in Great Britain by
DSPrint, Enfield

CONTENTS

2. Confronting ourselves

3. Special moments

4. Relationships

5. Illness and healing

6. Birth and death

Preface

If Jews have a deficiency in their prayers, it is that we tend to rely on those already laid out in the standard services rather than make up our own. Rarely do we pray impromptu, even in services. When on a Sabbath morning I tell congregants that "we pause a while and use the time for thoughts of our own", the regular turning of pages indicates that most prefer to stick with the written lines rather than wander off into more personal territory. This applies to rabbis too, and was brought home to me when doing an interview with a Christian radio programme. Just before it finished, the presenter said "Thank you Rabbi Romain; can you now end by leading us in a brief prayer". Christian ministers do impromptu prayers all the time, closing their eyes - on the radio, before a meeting, at a bedside - and invoking God for some cause. By contrast, rabbis generally pray at set times, and at which point they tend to take out their prayer book and turn to a particular page. As I had not expected such an invitation (nor brought a prayer book), I gaped at him momentarily, and then quickly resorted to quoting the *Oseh Shalom* in Hebrew and English. It worked, just, but it highlighted how unused we are to composing prayers at will. I realised why committed Christians talk of their 'prayer life' and Jews do not.

This book is an attempt to widen Jewish prayer life and to show that Jewish prayers can cover all situations, however personal and however messy, not just the official daily, Sabbath and festival set pieces. Moreover, these prayers have been composed anew, showing also that we do not have to 'go by the book' but can write our own prayers for a variety of circumstances. After all, when it comes to our own religious feelings and needs, we are each the experts. The success of this book, therefore, will be measured not only if you find some of the enclosed prayers meaningful, but if they also inspire you to compose your own, be it now or at some stage in the future.

The prayers in this book are written by twenty three different rabbis in all. They therefore differ widely in their style, their use of Hebrew, the way they address God, and whether they ask God to help us directly or ask God to inspire us to help ourselves. What the writers have in common is, first, that they are all members of the Assembly of Reform Rabbis UK; second, that they have identified a variety of needs that are not addressed in standard prayers books. Please note that these prayers are only offerings, not set in stone, with the main purpose of being helpful. So if the overall theme of a particular prayer is appropriate but certain lines do not fit your personal situation exactly, they can be omitted or varied so as to be right for you. For those who wish to delve into the Jewish concept of prayer, this booklet starts with a short essay containing some thoughts on the subject: why we pray, whether prayers work, what not to pray for and when to give up. Like the prayers in the pages following, it is a personal view, although rooted in Jewish tradition and shaped by years of leading services.

Thanks are due to all those who contributed prayers, some of which they had written of their own accord already and others which they composed specially for this book. Biographical details of them, along with who wrote what, are to be found at the back. The idea of the book came out of the annual *Kallah* (gathering) of Reform rabbis at Charney Manor in 2008 when we were discussing the new edition of Daily and Sabbath Prayer Book, *Forms of Prayer*, being issued that year. We thought of many other situations that needed addressing but which we could not fit into its pages and hence this publication to fill the gap. In fact, eight prayers from *Forms of Prayer* are included here as they compliment this book's themes so well. I am grateful to the Movement for Reform Judaism for its permission to reproduce them. References in footnotes to standard prayers are from that edition. I am also indebted to SCM Press for its permission to reproduce material that first appeared in its publications. Similarly to Liberal Judaism. Thanks are due also to Paul Freedman, Raymond Goldman and Sybil Sheridan for reading the proofs, and to Sylvia Morris for her technical assistance.

The choice of themes for the prayers that follow was dictated purely by those who wrote and submitted them. Many are concerned with the traumas and challenges we face, and tend to deal with the downside of life rather than its upside, although there are ones for joyous occasions too. Perhaps that says something about when we turn to personal prayer most. However, a note of hope permeates them all, along with a desire for personal renewal. I hope the book serves this purpose.

Jonathan Romain
September 2009

Jewish Prayer

The problem of prayer

Prayer is hard. There is an assumption that everyone ought to be able to pray, and that there is something wrong with us if we cannot do so. On the contrary, what is wrong is that assumption. It can be enormously difficult opening up, putting thoughts into words, expressing deep hopes or debilitating fears. It is significant that when the Hasidic rebbe, the Tzanzer, was asked what he did before praying, he replied "I pray that I may be able to pray properly". Personally, I have always taken great comfort from the saying of another rebbe, Mendel of Kotzk, who declared: "He who is about to pray should learn from a common labourer, who sometimes takes a whole day to prepare for a job. A wood cutter who spends most of the day sharpening his saw and only the last hour cutting the wood, has earned his day's wages". Few of us have that much time at our disposal, but the idea that success is not instant and often comes after periods of long preparation rings true.

Equally recognisable is the story about how the Baal Shem Tov once refused to enter a particular synagogue because it was "too full of prayers". When he saw the astonished reaction of his followers, he explained that so many routine and insincere prayers were being uttered there that they could not rise to heaven and stayed in the synagogue stifling the atmosphere. This is a long way from Abraham Joshua Heschel's remark that "Prayer is our humble answer to the inconceivable surprise of living". It shows that the experience of prayer can be both frustrating and inspirational, as well as several variations inbetween such extremes. It also proves how important it is not to be put off by the problems and still aim for the worthwhile aspects.

That is what makes the promise in the Book of Jeremiah so encouraging : "When you call Me and come and pray to Me, I will hear you. When you seek Me, you will find Me, if you search for Me with all your heart. I shall let you find Me, says the Eternal" (29:12-14). It is certainly an invitation worth taking up[1].

What is prayer ?

Let's go for the official answer first and then examine some alternative ones. According to Joseph Hertz, former Chief Rabbi and editor of the 'Hertz Chumash', prayer is "an instinct that springs eternally from man's unquenchable faith in a living God, almighty and merciful, who hears prayer and answers those who call upon Him in truth. It ranges from half-articulate confession of sin, to jubilant expression of joyful fellowship with God"[2] In other words, prayer is communion with God, a Jacob's ladder joining heaven to earth, men and women trying to establish a relationship with their Maker, seeking out the awesome presence that we cannot define but sense is there. It is an acknowledgement that there is something more to life than what we can see and touch and manipulate - something that dwarfs humanity and transcends history.

However, the idea of prayer being from humans to God is only part of the answer, with a Jewish understanding of prayer being much wider. This becomes obvious when you look at the different words we use. The English

---

[1] The quotations are to be found in the section 'Meditations before Prayer' in Forms of Prayer, London : Movement for Reform Judaism, 2008 pp. 10 - 26, which is worth reading in its entirety.

[2] Joseph Hertz in his Introduction to *The Daily Prayer Book*, London : Soncino, 1941

term 'to pray' comes from the Latin verb *precare*, meaning to entreat or supplicate, with the image of humans opening their hearts to God, arms open and on their knees (mentally if not physically). By contrast, the Hebrew term 'to pray' comes from Hebrew verb *l'hitpalleil*, meaning 'to judge oneself'. Here, prayer is an act of self-examination, not so much addressing God but oneself. This is most dramatically expressed in the prayer recited on Sabbath mornings, *Ribbon ha-olamim*, which asks: "What are we? What is our life? What is our love? What is our justice? What is our success? What is our endurance? What is our power?"[3]. I do not want to give the idea that Jewish prayer ignores God and is an act of personal therapy, but it does contain a strong element of looking at oneself in a critical way. Prayer-time can be the only occasion when we force ourselves to be objective, considering our existence and to what extent we live up to the ideals to which we say we subscribe, and resolving to lessen the gap between them.

Still, there are plenty of other reasons why people choose to pray. Some are thinking neither of God nor of themselves but have a sense of community. They feel that this is the way to express their Jewish identity, enjoying the camaraderie that arises from coming to synagogue, knowing that everyone else there has given up the opportunity of doing dozens of other activities so as to share time together and recreate the words and atmosphere in which past generations of Jews have engaged. It is no accident that some of the key parts of a service require there to be a *minyan* (quorum) of ten adults present: we can always pray by ourselves, but there can be particular advantages to communal prayers. We merge ourselves with the people of Israel - both those in our immediate congregation and the

[3] *Forms of Prayer*, ibid. p. 167

Jewish community worldwide - and become the sound of the family of Abraham.

Another motive for prayer is as a direct response to events that occur in our life: be it the desire to give thanks after a spot of good fortune, or for the fact that we are still alive and enjoying relative health and security despite the many things that could so easily have gone wrong. Less happily, it could be the need to turn somewhere at times of trauma or despair. As Abraham Lincoln - who was not a regular church-goer - put it : "I have been driven many times to my knees, by the overwhelming conviction that I had nowhere else to go".

What is remarkable is that the Hebrew word for prayer is only used a handful of times in the entire Five Books of Moses. One reason might be that biblical figures do not pray to God in a ritualised sense, but just talk to God. It is more of a conversation that an act of imploring, with a sense that God is immediate and approachable. That is why the *Midrash* (rabbinic lore) holds that one of the first instances of prayer concerned the discussion about Sodom and Gomorrah, when Abraham demands of God: "Will You really sweep away the righteous with the wicked? Perhaps there are fifty righteous men in the city...Far be it from You to act in such a way and slay the righteous with the wicked...Shall not the Judge of all the earth do justly?" (Genesis 18:23-5). This is not a prayer but a rant, a confrontation, an argument, with Abraham addressing God as if on equal terms. It is very far from the idea of us being snivelling wretches who can only cringe in God's presence. Abraham respects God, but does not grovel before God. So with us: we may exist only because of the light of God - but we can sparkle back at God.

It is significant that this theme is not just found in the Bible but continues in subsequent Jewish life. Another famous example is Rabbi Levi

Yitzhak of Berdichev, the eighteenth century Polish Hasidic leader. It is said that one *Yom Kippur*, towards the end of the service as nightfall was approaching and the 'gates of mercy' were about to close, he put down his prayer book, went up to the Ark and addressed God: "Let us examine what has happened over the past year. We have sinned...we have committed many faults...we have done wrong. But what about You? There have been earthquakes and harvest failures and droughts. You have created famine and caused disease to flourish. Widows and orphans have multiplied because of You. It seems that You have not done so well either. Let us make a deal. We shall forgive You if You forgive us". And apparently his request was granted! As with Abraham, here is prayer that both acknowledges and challenges God. Perhaps it is too individualistic a style to be used on the printed pages of the prayer book, but is certainly appropriate for personal prayer. On that subject, it is worth noting that while personal prayer could mean saying formal prayers at home from the book, garbed in a *kippah* (head-covering) and *tallit* (prayer-shawl), it can also mean reciting impromptu prayers of our own, or being silent in deep reflection, or bursting into song, or humming a hum, or whistling or dancing - whatever expresses our hopes and fears and desires and moods. As with Abraham and Levi Yitzhak, it can be a matter of talking *with* God, as did Tevye the Milkman, chatting away, keeping God in touch with what was going on, consulting God, occasionally advising God and even quoting "the Good Book" at God. Although Tevye was only a fictional character, his easy relationship with God epitomised one that many people share, or would like to share.

To whom are we praying ?

It is helpful to check as to whom we are directing our prayers. Simply saying "God" is not enough as there are so many different versions of God in the Bible and we may identify with one in particular rather than with the others, or hold together more than one at a time, or vacillate between them, or find different images appropriate at different stages in our lives. The point is, though, that all are aspects of God and we need not feel obliged to fit into a theological straight-jacket but can relate to God in our own way : there is God the Creator, the First Cause that set the world in motion, that was responsible for life as we know it, and it does not matter whether it was through Adam and Eve or though the amoeba, but somehow, somewhere there was a creative force which, for short, we call God. Then there is God the Revealer, who not only established the world but intervened in its affairs, condemning Cain for the murder he committed, saving Noah for his righteousness, who makes the Divine will known and bids that we follow it. Then there is the Jewish God who made a covenant with Abraham, declared that Israel was God's "first-born" and chose Israel for a special role. It is the God with whom we have a special family connection, our God and the God of our ancestors.

There is also the personal God, who not only does majestic acts but who also has a relationship with individual men and women. The God who can enter into the lives of ordinary people and allow them to communicate with something so much greater than themselves. There is the inner God, who came to Elijah not in the wind, not in the earthquake, not in the fire but in the small still voice; and so with us, who speaks through the silent promptings of our conscience, who is within us, a Divine element to which we choose to pay attention or ignore. Amid these roles, God can be the fierce judge or the best friend, the distant law-giver or the intimate lover. All these are the same God, but which show themselves at different times, like ice, hail, water and snow all being manifestations of the same essence.

While other faiths have had internal wars and sectarian heresies over the right or wrong belief as to the nature of God, Judaism never sought to tie down God in the same way. That is why, alongside the concepts above, it is also possible to have very different mental pictures of God: God as puppeteer who pulls the strings, controls the world and orders our lives; or, the exact opposite, God the watch-maker, who puts the world together, winds it up, and then stands back to leave it to run of its own accord; or God the check-out operator at a supermarket till; we spend our time going up the aisles, taking this, ignoring that, doing what we want, but eventually we have to come to the exit and God adds up the sum of our life; or God the source of nature, the regularity of day and night, the changing of the seasons, the world we expect to still be there every morning when we wake. All are the Jewish God, or the God of the Jews – and the reason Judaism can be so relaxed about it is because it is a form of arrogance to say we know exactly what God is and is not, and that we can define God. Perhaps the best we can do with any certainty is to talk of our own relationship with God, how it is or how we would like it to be.

For what are we praying ?

In the set liturgy of the Prayer Book, there are three main types of prayer - petition, praise and thanksgiving (although, as we have seen above, personal prayer can encompass a much wider range of types, from 'keeping in touch' to expressing confusion or anger). Prayers of petition present an immediate philosophical challenge: if God is omniscient and knows everything, then God knows what we need before we do, so why do we have to tell God in the first place? This can lead to a lot of speculation over the notion of pre-determination. Thus if God has determined that a person's prayer will be granted, why bother uttering it? Conversely, if God has determined that it not be granted, then saying the prayer will not have any effect and is pointless. However, as the Bible so often reminds us, what is important is not what God needs to know, but what we have to realise. So when God asks Adam in the garden of Eden "Where are you?" (Genesis 3:9), the object is not to inform God but for Adam to assess his own position.

It is right and natural, therefore, to pray for what we really want - not just for the noble aspirations we think we ought to want, but for what our heart desires. This means thinking of oneself - and there is no reason why prayer should not be selfish so long as it is not entirely selfish and also makes room for the needs of others. So, prayers can range from general desires such as happiness or health, or more specific concerns. This is epitomised by the story of the synagogue whose shofar blower died shortly before the High Holy Days, with the result that the community needed a replacement urgently. A number of applicants applied, all musically very able, and in order to distinguish between them, the rabbi asked them what they would be thinking about when they blew the shofar over the New Year. One replied, "I shall concentrate on the tremendous responsibility I have to get the notes right". Another said, "I will remind myself how holy is the moment and how awesome is the occasion". A third responded, "I shall be thinking of my three children whom I struggle to feed and clothe, and hope that God will help". The rabbi selected the latter, on the grounds that he would blow the shofar with the greatest sense of urgency and power.

But whilst we can ask God for whatever we want, it is wiser not to pray for the impossible, for magical tricks to alter reality or change circumstances. Far better to pray for the possible, for ways of dealing with reality and for qualities to help face circumstances. When faced with a major crisis, at home or at work, there is little point in praying for it to suddenly disappear in a puff of smoke, but instead to ask for the strength to tackle it properly. So rather than imploring "Please God give me a lucky break with my sales record at work", try "Please God give me the insight to see how I can improve and the determination to succeed". When, to cite a situation so many people have to face, someone close to us is on their death-bed and is clearly fading away, then it is probably better not to pray for a last-minute miracle-cure but that they should be able to face death calmly and that we have the courage to carry on without them. That way we both strengthen ourselves and also, just as importantly, do not build likely failure into our prayers that then leave us demoralised just at the time when we are most under stress. After all, we would urge a schoolchild facing exams the next day not to pray that they be cancelled, but for the ability to think clearly - in other words, for personal qualities not unrealistic expectations.

Of course, this is not a new topic and the rabbis of the Middle Ages had to battle against unrealistic prayers in their time too, for we are told that "To pray for the impossible is disgraceful. It is as if one had brought into a shed a hundred measures of corn and prayed - May it be Your will that they become two hundred" (*Tosefta, Berachot* 7). In fact the very first rabbinic texts indicate that even the earliest rabbis pondered over how not to pray. In the fifth century the Talmud was keen to discourage would-be martyrs or self-haters and declared that we may not pray that good fortune be taken away from us. The thinking behind this was that self-affliction is not healthy for the individual concerned, plus the fact that such a person would no doubt end up being a burden on everyone else (*Ta'anit* 22a).

There was also a strong concept of prayers that are in vain and that should never be made in the first place : "If a man's wife is pregnant and he says, 'God grant that my wife bear a male child', this is in vain [as its gender is already determined]. If he is coming home from a journey and hears cries of distress in the town and says, 'God grant that it is not from my house', this is a vain prayer [for it already is or is not]"(*Berachot* 54a). The rabbis also addressed another type of prayer that was equally instinctive but which they ruled was out of order: castigating our enemies, even when they are highly unpleasant. Praying for the death of the wicked was prohibited - instead we are only to pray for the destruction of wickedness. Thus we should concentrate on ending evil rather than eliminating the individuals who commit evil. After all, says the Zohar, if God had killed the idolater Terah, then his son Abraham may never have been born and there would have been no Israel, no Torah and no prophets.

Does God answer prayer ?

It should be stated that not all Jews believe in a God who responds to individuals. As indicated above, God is the power behind the universe, responsible for the amazing world around us and the life we ourselves have. For some Jews, though, that God does not take a personal interest in the millions of people that exist. God's awesome greatness was in starting the process, not supervising the results. They are therefore happy to give thanks to God for our existence, and see purpose in coming to synagogue both for the sake of camaraderie with others and as a way of reinforcing communal values. But they do not expect to receive an audience with God or to be heard from afar. This is not seen as a disappointment, but simply a fact. For them, God cannot both span the stellar system and tune in to their particular voice. For others, though, the glory of God is that God is both transcendent and immanent, far above us, yet approachable.

As to whether God answers prayer, one response is 'sometimes'. Sometimes our prayers seem to be successful and what we had dared to hope for comes to pass, whereas other times our prayers seem to have no effect at all. Still, that is looking at it from the simplistic yardstick of "what I wanted did or did not happen". Another way of looking at it is that prayer is always answered, but it may be the response is "no". This begs the question of whether God is being capricious by granting some prayers and not others, however sincerely requested and however worthy the petitioner. Two explanations leap forward. One is that although we are praying for what we believe will benefit us, in reality it may not be so desirable, and might even be harmful in ways we cannot foresee. To give a dramatic example, think of those who have been stuck in a traffic jam on their way to the airport, prayed passionately that they did not miss the flight, did miss it, but then were mightily relieved when they learnt that the plane had crashed. The other possibility is that one person's prayer may conflict with that of another person. So if a farmer and umbrella-maker are standing next to each other in synagogue, the former praying for sunshine and the later for rain, one of them is going to be disappointed.

The example is often given of a fly that lands on a blob of paint on a Rembrandt. The fly cannot see any purpose to that blob and views it merely as an obstruction to its progress. But a human being who observes the painting from a distance knows that without that particular blob, the picture would be incomplete. It is an example that can be both intensely annoying and very helpful, depending on our mood at the time. In similar vein is the suggestion that we look at one side of an embroidery and see an incoherent mess, but turn over to the other side and a wonderful scene is depicted. Both are true in that there is much in life which frustrates us and against which we rail, but our perspective is limited and our prayers might be different if we could see the overall picture. That is not, however, a recipe for complacency and meekly to accept whatever comes our way. There may be every reason to be upset or angry - for ourselves or on behalf of others - and even if the long-term outcome may be unknowable, we can still pray for change, and take actions to make it happen as well. Precisely because we do not know what the future holds, we have to try to fashion it as we think best. Prayer can be one method, and as Tennyson urges us to remember, "More things are wrought by prayer/Than this world dreams of. Wherefore let thy voice/Rise like a fountain night and day"[4].

Even if the particular petition we make is not granted - and this also applies to those who do not believe in a God who responds to individuals in the first place - the prayer may still be of benefit in a number of ways. It has forced us to focus on our needs and articulate our hopes. It has clarified thoughts and shown the direction in which we should go. It has made us aware of our limitations, engendered the humility to ask for help and brought to the fore the depth of character that will enable us to face those challenges. It can bring a sense of release from having addressed God and unburdened ourselves. As the poet George Meredith expressed it : 'The person who rises from prayer a better man, his prayer is answered"[5].

---

[4] Alfred Tennyson, *Morte D'Arthur,* l. 247-9

[5] Quoted in Louis Jacobs, *Jewish Prayer*, London : Jewish Chronicle Publications, 1962. I am indebted to the book for several literary and rabbinic quotations.

What is the point of giving praise ?

The second of the three traditional types of prayer - petition, praise and thanks - seems simple enough. It is typified by the *Kaddish* which urges us to "bless...extol...tell aloud...raise aloft...set on high...honour...exalt...and praise the Holy One whose name is blessed". You cannot get much more emphatic than that. However, here too difficult questions arise. One is: who are we to praise God? How do those who are finite and mortal address a God who is infinite and eternal? Anything we utter is bound to be inadequate and will fall short of God's true greatness. On the other hand, to say nothing and appear to ignore God's glory would be equally wrong. So the answer is to go ahead with our praises, but with the mental reservation that they are only attempts and can never be fully descriptive. Hence the *Aleinu* prayer starts off by declaring "It is our duty to praise the Ruler of all, to recognise the greatness of the Creator of first things...". But another difficulty is that we inevitably think of God in human terms. That is the limited range of our vocabulary. It carries the danger of over-humanising God, a tendency that led Voltaire to write: "God created man in his own image, and man returned the compliment". Yet Judaism has always veered away from the Greeks and Romans who not only gave their deities human characteristics (including vices such as jealousy, lust and intoxication) but even sculpted them with human bodies. The Jewish God is incorporeal, without form, beyond depiction and cannot be captured in a neat phrase.

Yet, despite this, we are still stuck with the fact that the human mind can only relate its own experiences. The Bible has frequent anthropomorphisms, with God "walking in the garden of Eden", "covering Moses with His hand", "sitting on a throne" (Genesis 22:8; Exodus 33:22; Isaiah 6:1). No wonder that many a synagogue Ark has the Hebrew inscription on it "Know before whom you stand". It is a combination of trying to understand who/what God is, but also who/what God is not. Moreover, for many people, what is important is not so much defining the nature of God, but establishing a relationship with God. This formed the basis of the teachings of Martin Buber, who wrote on the value of an 'I-Thou' relationship over that of an 'I-It' relationship. The latter is about usefulness, the former is a matter of intimacy. The complexity of being both in awe of God yet in touch with God at the same time - of being a puny part of the universe yet also the centre of God's attention - is expressed by the curious format of the Hebrew of most blessings : "Blessed are You [second person, with a sense of the familiar] our Living God, Sovereign of the universe, who has sanctified us by His commandments [third person, much more distant]..." It highlights that we can know God through God's deeds, but we cannot know God's essence. As Joseph Hertz put it, "we know God from the footprint He leaves behind in human history, like a ship that has passed over the horizon and disappeared from sight but whose wake is still visible".

This in turn begs the question that if our efforts at praise are bound to be so inadequate, what is the point of them? One answer is that more than God needs to receive them, we need to give them. It turns our mind to high ideals. By speaking of God as merciful, compassionate and just, we remind ourselves that such qualities are worth making our own. It reinforces the notion that we should strive to be God-like. It brings to the fore the biblical command of *imitatio dei*, that "You shall be holy, for I the Eternal your God am holy" (Leviticus 19:2). For some, there is a deeper aspect to it. God may exist independently of humans, but unless humans recognise God's existence, then God does not exist for them. This daring idea, that God depends on humans, is expressed in the ancient midrashic text *Pesikta de*

Rav Kahana in which Rabbi Shimon bar Yochai comments on the biblical phrase, "You are My witnesses, says the Eternal One and I am God" : "This means: if you give witness to Me, then I am the Eternal One. But if you are not My witnesses, then I am not the Eternal One".

Do I have to thank God ?

If prayers of praise reflect the nature and power of God, prayers of thanks are for what we enjoy and benefit from personally. Some of them speak of how God's qualities affect us communally, others are more personal. As with the prayers of praise, the motivation is more for our own need to express them than God's need to hear them. They produce a heightened sense of awareness of the marvels of life that we tend to appreciate only when we are in danger of losing them. They remind us to take delight in what seems so commonplace and mundane: to sense the mystery in the rising and setting of the sun, appreciate the goodness in the bread we eat, value the water we drink. They help lift the ordinary to the extraordinary and see afresh what is so easy to take for granted. As Elizabeth Barrett Browning put it: "Earth's crammed with heaven, / And every common bush afire with God; / But only he who sees, takes off his shoes, / The rest sit round it, and pluck blackberries". Such prayers also remind us that life is to be enjoyed rather than denied. There is no reason why we should not take advantage of all the material benefits and pleasures available to us, so long as they do not result in us harming ourselves or doing so at the expense of others. As the Talmud tells us, in the world to come a person will be held accountable for every good thing from which we might have benefited but ignored.

But what happens when we have feelings less positive than thanksgiving? When we have been hurt by people, bruised by the world or feel let down by God. One reaction is simply to accept misfortune - either (from a determinist point of view) as the will of God or (from a free-will perspective) as the way things have turned out. It finds expression in the remarkable benediction that appears counter-intuitive: a blessing upon hearing bad news. Whereas one might expect to rage against bad news, we are urged to come to terms with it: "Blessed are You, our Living God, Sovereign of the Universe, the true judge". But there is another response. Rather than submit to the way of the world, we can protest about it and rebel against what God has caused or (depending on our attitude) has allowed to happen. Thus Honi Ha'Magel refused to accept the drought that was causing so much suffering in first century Israel. He drew a circle around himself and told God that he would refuse to budge from the circle until God made it rain. So it rained. We may not have such powers, but other avenues are open to us in confronting the problems of our age - be it prayer or action or both - that seek to improve the world we inhabit so that we can thank God and do not have to omit certain prayers because they stick in our throat.

Difficulties with prayer need not mean avoidance or denial. The ability to express our darker emotions - be it disappointment, frustration or anger - is important. Otherwise it is not a full and open relationship. That is why David was not afraid to vent his distress in prayer, complaining "Why have You forgotten me ? Why must I go about mournfully, oppressed by my enemies ?" (Psalm 42:10). He knew that it is perfectly natural to be angry; the real question is what do we do with our anger? How do we channel it from hurting others or poisoning ourselves, and turn aggressive energy to constructive purposes ? It is an issue that confronts us every time we say the paragraph that is sometimes included at the end of the Thanksgiving after Meals: "I have been young and am now grown old, and have never seen a righteous person forsaken" (Psalm 37:25). One tradition is to read it silently, because it is not true and many righteous people do suffer; another tradition is to say it out aloud because we want to hasten the time when it is true and so we remind ourselves of the personal challenge to make it so.

Is prayer obligatory ?

There is a problem with our adherence to set times for prayer, be it midweek, Sabbath or festivals. Surely if prayer is to be meaningful it has to be voluntary. Yet Jewish tradition also sees it as a duty, irrespective of what mood we are in. Maimonides includes the obligation to pray as one of the 613 commandments, deriving it from "And you shall serve the Eternal your God" (Exodus 23:25). This might seem to detract from the sincerity of prayer, but it could be argued that praying is our natural instinct anyway, as well as being therapeutic for us, and that Judaism is just providing a structure and discipline through which we can fulfil the desire to communicate with God. Of course, even though there are set times, that does not prevent us from praying at additional times whenever we so wish. That choice also applies to the language in which we pray. Once Hebrew was no longer the vernacular for many Jews, there were clamourings for prayers to be said in the mother-tongue, which is why a number of prayers were composed in Aramaic from the second century onwards. Famous examples range from the *Kaddish* to *Kol Nidre* to *Had Gadya*. When the issue is discussed in the Talmud, the verdict is that communal prayers can be in the vernacular but private prayers must be in Hebrew (*Sotah* 32b). However, a minority opinion held that the reverse should be the pattern, and this is what became customary until the birth of Reform Judaism in the mid-nineteenth century.

The advantage of using the vernacular is two-fold : first, enabling those who do not have command of Hebrew to be able to participate; second, so that all can understand the words they are saying. After all, when Moses proclaimed the Ten Commandments or David wrote his psalms in Hebrew, they were not doing so because it was a holy tongue but because it was their natural language. However, there are also powerful arguments for keeping a degree of Hebrew in the service too. One is that passages are usually best in the original language in which they were written, and so Hebrew prayers carry associations and resonate in a way that is lost in translation. Another factor is that, for Jews, Hebrew is a universal language, so that if a Jew from England visits a synagogue in Japan and stands next to someone from Russia, both will be able to join in the service and feel equally at home. It might also be added that, for some, the attraction of Hebrew is precisely because they can read it but not understand it. They may not actually agree with what the translation says - after all the prayer was written by someone else in a totally different era - but they can invest in the Hebrew sounds what they feel and use them as a vehicle for what they cannot articulate fully in English.

Is it better praying with others or by myself ?

If prayer is intensely personal, why the Jewish emphasis on communal prayer ? As so often, this is not a new discussion, and was long ago pre-empted in the Talmud. During a debate on the subject, Rabbi Isaac states that communal prayer is inherently superior because it is accompanied by the Divine presence. His proof is that "God stands in the congregation of the godly" (Psalm 82:1). Whether one argues that this is defined as a quorum of ten adult males (the Orthodox interpretation) or of ten Jews (the Reform attitude), either way there is a clear preference for praying with others. However, Rav Ashi cites another biblical verse to prove that God's presence is also with a single individual : "In every place I cause My name to be mentioned, I will come to you and bless you" (Exodus 20:24). So which mode is preferable ? The Talmud decides that both are valid but "To a synagogue gathering, the Divine presence comes first, and to an individual it only comes afterwards" (*Berachot* 6a).

It is certainly true that communal prayer has many benefits. A pragmatic one is the discipline it brings - because others expect us to be there, we go; whereas without this structure and with so many other distractions at hand, it might be very easy for things to slip away and our prayer time simply not happen. Another factor is that it can lead to a heightened atmosphere: through being with others our own personal mood is lifted up on a wing of communal prayer and can be imbued with an extra zest it would not otherwise have by itself. Conversely, our presence can help others, and those who came feeling tired or despondent can be reinvigorated or cheered by the mood that we help create by being there. Although we each go to a service hoping to gain from it in some way, we also ought - to adapt a slogan - to 'think not of what the rest of congregation can do for us, but of what we can do for the rest of congregation'. By way of reinforcing the point, Rabbi Isaac raises the stakes and declares that "If a person is accustomed to attend synagogue regularly and one day he does not go, the Holy Blessed One makes inquiry after him" (*Berachot* 6b). In fact, it is a double-edged statement: on the one hand, it implies that if we are absent, we are not only letting down our neighbour but disappointing God; on the other hand it hints that synagogue absenteeism was long an issue and rabbis were always seeking ways of combating it!

Still, much as there are advantages to communal prayers, everyone has their own personal needs, and there is nearly always a part of the service where there is a period of silence to provide time for our private thoughts. The fact that many people at this point just carry on reading the printed prayers suggests that many of us have lost the ability to pray personally.
We may pray in times of extremity, such as facing danger - which is then more an urgent cry for help - but many of us are not at ease talking to God without the crutch of set passages. This is all the more regrettable given that, historically, congregational prayer was a late development. Personal prayers came first. Most of the early biblical figures prayed alone, not with family or friends. It was rarely in unison with others, with a notable exception being the Song of the Sea (Exodus 15). But given the emphasis on community, if we are unable to attend one of the statutory services - for instance, on Sabbath evening - but want to recite it ourself at home, a lovely tradition is to do so at the same time that the community would be starting its prayers. It means that even if we are separate from them physically, we are at one with them spiritually, and identifying with them.

How do I pray ?

Sometimes the seemingly obvious is not at all obvious. Of course we can open the prayer book at the first page and start reading, but, as we have seen, the point is not to get to the foot of the page but to mean what we are reading. That is why the rabbis put such emphasis on *kavvanah* (concentration) so that we really engage with what the prayers are saying, with our mind thinking what our lips are reciting. Of course the fact that the rabbis frequently mention this is only because it is so easy to do the opposite - read the text, but let our mind wander off and go on liturgical autopilot. Part of the reason for Reform reducing the Sabbath morning service from three or four hours and restoring it to the original much shorter length was to allow people to concentrate. Better to pray for an hour sincerely than to sit there for several hours aimlessly. Even an hour's solid concentration can be a hard task, and it is common to find we have reached the end of a paragraph without remembering a word of it because our thoughts have gone elsewhere. In that case, just get back to the service and pick up the theme; what counts is what we do concentrate on, not what we have missed. In fact, when the rabbis were asked whether a person who had read a prayer without thinking about it should go back and repeat it, they were realistic enough to accept that we cannot maintain constant religious highs. They only asked that a certain minimum had been achieved and, remarkably, they defined that as the first line of the *Shema* and the opening paragraph of the *Amidah*. Moreover, they were not thinking just of others, but also of themselves. In a remarkable discussion in the Jerusalem Talmud, Rabbi Hiyya said he had never managed to concentrate fully for an entire service while Shmuel admitted his mind often wandered and he found himself counting the clouds (*Berachot* 2:4, 16a). This is not permission to deliberately skip parts of the service, but it does mean we do not have to feel overly-guilty if we find that chunks of it pass us by.

There are also other ways of achieving *kavvanah* rather than forcing ourselves to focus on the prayers at hand. One is to study the history and development of Jewish prayer, so that the words on the pages resonate with more meaning. It makes it much more significant when we realise, for instance, that the *Ma Tovu* is not composed from original material but the result of someone weaving together several verses from different books of the Bible; moreover, it is done in such a way that the words match our physical actions as we enter synagogue. Another method is to concentrate on a different prayer each time we attend synagogue, so that we gradually come to terms with successive ones and build up ownership of the service as a whole. Alternatively, instead of just arriving at synagogue and seeing what happens, we can decide in advance to focus on a particular theme - our health, our business, our goals - or on the welfare of a particular person we know, and this may give our prayers more depth and purpose.

Some people find that wearing a 'prayer uniform' helps get them in the mood of prayer and separates them from any distractions. This could involve donning a *kippah, tallit* or *tefillin* (prayer-boxes), and is one of the reasons why Reform has extended their usage to women as part of the general principle of equality in worship. Another option is to think on what the act of prayer implies and how awesome is the attempt to address God in person. If that leads to musing about the nature of God, the world and humanity, then that is prayer time well spent! It is like the story of the Apter Rebbe who started praying with others around him, but by the time they had finished he had not even got past the first page. When they asked him if he was alright, he replied "Yes, I started praying well, but when I came to the line 'I give thanks before You', I thought : 'who am I to give thanks to God ?' and have been thinking about it ever since". Conversely, it may be realistic to suggest that there should be a time-limit to unsuccessful attempts at personal prayer: it might be better to admit it, stop and try again another time. Bashing our head against a brick wall can be as useless with prayers as it is with anything else if they are simply leading nowhere.

Leo Baeck used to say that even if one could not observe the whole of the Sabbath, one should at least strive to have some Sabbath moments. Perhaps the same is true of prayer; many of us are unlikely to have long periods of spiritual piety, but we can have moments of prayer when we feel we are in touch with God, or at one with those around us, or exploring the deepest part of ourselves. Those moments are worth praying for.

Jonathan Romain

1. Situations that test us

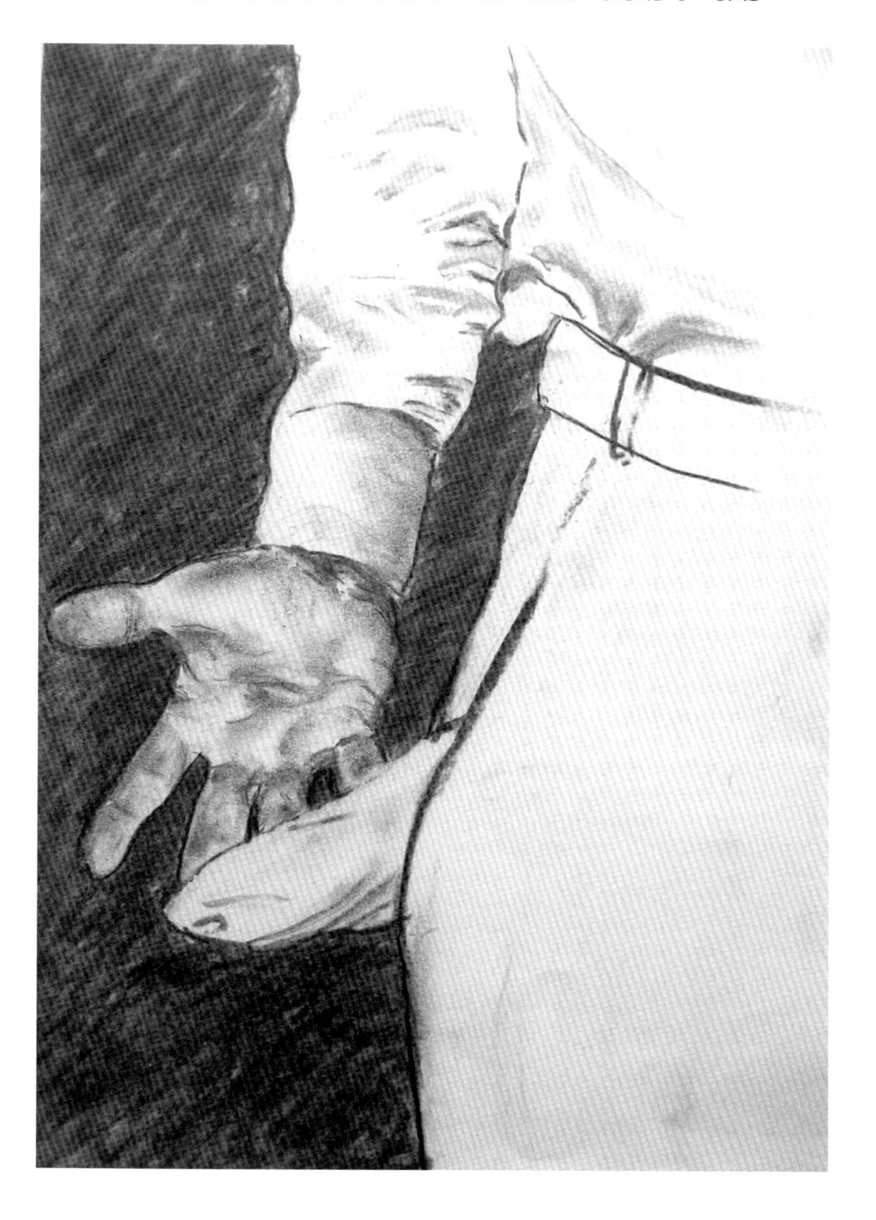

Before an exam

My God, I know how much I have prepared for the exam I am about to take. And how little I know. How little any of us can ever know. And yet I have confidence: in my own abilities, and in the wisdom within me, which no exam can measure. I trust that I will do the best I can, and that Your presence will be with me as I test what I can do. I trust too that I can come to understand that my success or failure now is not the measure of who I am, or what I will become. Life examines us every day, tests us to the limit: how generous are we? How loving? How much does a passion for justice stir our souls? How much do we care for those around us, and this fragile world we all inhabit? Help us not to forget that these are the questions that really count. Help us not to cheat when we examine our lives in the years to come.

And meanwhile – help me now to achieve some small success in the days ahead. Keep me calm, and confident, trusting in what I know, trusting in You, trusting in the support of family and friends whatever will result in the fullness of time.

Before an exam - for a parent

As my child studies, not as hard as I would like
Or struggles pale and myopic into the night
I ask You God – let children find pleasure in study
And let them enjoy the learning they acquire
And not think only of the grades
Or the gateway this examination will open or close.
I remember them as a baby, when every achievement: a smile, a grasp, a word was truly valued.
I remember them as a child finding out about the world with pleasure and awe.
I remember vowing not to let the world hurt them, not to let the judgment of the world curtail their own selves
So let me remember what is truly important now
And have confidence that what will be will open up the future in the right way
For the miracle that is my child

Before a driving test

Oh God, who watches the steps of every living being
And who knows the thoughts of each of us
Who made the earth by Your power and who established the world by Your wisdom
I ask for Your loving watchfulness as I prepare for this test.
I long for the freedom and possibilities that this license will provide me
Yet I know that I shall be in charge of a powerful force which can bring about death as well as enrich life
I pray that I am ready to take on this challenge. That my learning and my practice are enough
That I shall never be so arrogant as to say – "My power and My actions are all I need to think about"
But I shall care for all who cross my path
I shall look and observe and always care for those around me
And remember that while some trust in vehicles and others in their own skill
I shall know that life is fragile and precious and to be enjoyed with care and attention.
I will remember that my every action matters, that I must be present and concentrate every moment as I drive.
Help me to keep this before me always so that I will become a safe and thoughtful driver now and in the future.[6]

---

[6] the prayer contains oblique references to Deuteronomy 8:17; Ps 20:8; Jeremiah 51:15 and 51:21

Before a major sporting event

Sport, like religion, is another world in which to live. At its best it illuminates a dimension of being we long to glimpse: we hope to witness moments of inspiration and wonder, and poetry in motion, unfolding before our eyes. We rejoice in what the human body can do and the spirit of all being that animates those who compete.

We know the ways in which winning and losing seem to matter to us – and of course we hope that those we support will win this time around. But we know too that who wins or loses matters not a jot. Hope and despair, success and failure – this is the stuff of life, and the stuff of sport, that mirrors life. There is no knowing what life, or sport, will next reveal: so let us enjoy the honest endeavour of the dramas yet to come, secure in the knowledge that even defeat can teach us what we need to learn – that loss is part of life, and victory is short-lived, and the game of life is a mystery through and through.

On making an investment

May "all kinds of fruitfulness be for good"[7]. Eternal God, as I commit the fruitfulness with which You have blessed me to .... may I do so for the good of those whom I love for now and the future.

May I invest with consciousness that You have given humankind the Earth to steward in all of its fullness. As we enjoy its fruits we must ensure that we do so with care for all of Your creation now and into the future. In investing in .... I am Your partner in bringing prosperity to Your creation and I am also Your partner in providing "enough food for all"[8] and in ensuring a sustainable future and a hope. May I have the courage to reason with those businesses in which I hold a stake to help their work to be more closely aligned to Yours as You guide the world into the future.

May Your favour be upon me to support me in the work I do and may its success be for the good of all.[9]

---

[7] from the *Amidah* in the Daily Service, *Forms of Prayer* p. 79
[8] from the Thanksgiving after Meals, *Forms of Prayer* p. 467
[9] Adapted from Psalm 90:17

On losing a job

"Sing to the Eternal a new song"[10]. A new life is opening in front of me. I have given a great deal of myself to my work at .....up to now. What I have given has been received and the reward that I have in turn received for my labours has supported me up until now. Now I leave that part of my life behind and ready myself for change.

In my life I have experienced changes and losses as I move from one phase to another. Each change has led me further on life's journey with the new road opened bringing me gains as I leave the losses behind.

Now I must find a new song to sing with the courage to step forward with the burden of regret and resentment left as far behind as I possibly can. It may be that in the coming years I will look upon this change with delight as its benefits become clear to me. It may be that I will need to change the way in which I enjoy life if work becomes of necessity a lesser part of my identity. Whatever the future turns out to be, I ask You my Living God to be with me on my journey. May the road of life ahead be full of fulfilment, guided by Your commandments.

"May it be Your will, my Living God that You guide me towards peace and lead me to my desired destination - to life, joy and peace"[11]

---

[10] Psalm 96:1
[11] From the Prayer for a Journey, *Forms of Prayer* p. 413

During unemployment

My God, You are the One who is said to support us all, the Rock on whom we can rely in times of trial. You give us the strength to face each day anew. Now that I am without work I realise how much meaning it gave to my life. And how bereft I feel without its routines and rituals, its financial recompense and its emotional rewards. Help me to be robust and resolute as I look for work again. I know my own abilities and strengths, and yet I know too that the world of work is unpredictable and clouded with uncertainty. This can unsettle me day and night, and upset my deepest hopes.

And so I turn to You, secure in the knowledge that You will accompany my journey in the days ahead. No one knows what the future holds, or what opportunities will cross my path. But no encounter in our lives lacks hidden significance: whatever the frustrations we face, there are opportunities for doing Your work at every moment of our lives. Our daily acts of kindness, of generosity and care, bring You into the world. This too is work, *avodah*, this service of God: the work of redemption which is never complete. It is our task amidst the vicissitudes of life, woven into our days, while our search for employment goes on. With renewed hope we embrace what is to come: "May the favour of the Eternal be upon us, to uphold us in the work we do, and support our work that is still to be done" [12]

---

[12] Based on Psalm 90:17

On bankruptcy

"You grant human beings knowledge and teach mortals understanding. Favour us with the knowledge, understanding and discernment that come from You".[13]

My God and God of my ancestors I speak to You at this terrible time. I have lost all that I have worked to realise and I feel that I have failed. All that made me safe and secure is gone from me. I am lost and I feel rejected and I am ashamed. How can I stand before You and before my fellow human beings? Let me hear Your voice of hope for the future and give me the spirit to hold fast to myself through this time. Help me to know that this is not the end of all things. You search me O God and know my heart and You understand all things. I offer this prayer to You for myself and for all those I love, not for the return of all my material possessions but that I may hold fast to You and come through this time. Teach me that this ending can be a new beginning and in Your mercy give me the strength to continue.

"Blessed are You, God, who favours us with knowledge". [14]

---

[13] From the *Amidah* in the Daily Service, *Forms of Prayer* p. 77
[14] idem

On retirement

God of the spirits of all living creatures. You alone understand the many changes we meet in the course of our life on Earth.

As I pass from one active stage to another I turn to You, grateful for what I have achieved, anticipating all that still lies before me.

Let no regrets about the past or anxieties about the future overwhelm me. Let me not be complacent or resigned, as if my life was already completed.

"The soul You have given me is pure" [15] and is renewed within me each waking day. May I also find renewal each day as I enter yet another stage and face once again the mystery of what lies before me.

May I not become a burden to others, but accept and welcome help when I need it. May I keep friendships of the past and find new ones in the life ahead. May I gain strength from those I love, and be able to give to them in return.

"May these my words,
and these hopes in my heart,
be acceptable to You,
O God, my Rock and my Redeemer" [16]

---

[15] From the Daily Service, *Forms of Prayer* p. 33
[16] Psalm 19:15

2. Confronting ourselves

An insomniac's prayer

"Safe and sound I lie down and sleep; for You keep me secure, Eternal One, alone"[17]. The words provoke and mock – my sleeplessness defies belief, the hours of darkness offer no relief, my restlessness disrupts the night, disturbs the dawn, denuding each new day of hope. This unsubtle derangement of the senses, this unwilled wakefulness – what purpose does it serve? I cannot but review my life, re-live the best and worst, the petty and the mean, the hurts I've caused and the hurts received, the grief I've known, the bleakness borne, the losses I've endured. Anxieties that never seem to end. To whom can I turn for solace in the silence of the night?

I wait and wonder where salvation lies. How many false dreams have I fashioned in my life? How many illusions have I entertained? False hopes abound, so where does hope reside for me? Amidst the mind's disquiet, can I open my heart and wait for You to enter in? Let this be my prayer, if I am to pray at all: that my hopefulness be rooted in what is true and lasts from age to age. "I lie down and sleep and wake again, for the Eternal One sustains me" [18]. What if this, perchance, were true? That, nurtured by You, I can feel secure, despite the randomness of life? Can I sense the Eternal in the endless night? The stillness I seek is within me now. Can the still small silent voice of life be whispering its blessing inside me once again? I hear the echo of the Psalmist's faith: You alone keep me secure. Let me lie down and sleep, Eternal One, cradled in Your care, my spirit calmed, comforted by Your compassion for my conflicted soul. Let me sleep secure, and let me wake refreshed, tucked into the silent presence of Your sustaining mystery.

---

[17] Psalm 4:9
[18] Psalm 3:6

Anxiety

"Heal us O God and we shall be healed; save us and we shall be saved. It is You that we praise. Send relief and healing for all our diseases and our sufferings and our wounds". [19]

Almighty God I speak to You out of my distress and confusion. I am very afraid and I do not know why. There is panic rushing around inside me. I know that You are always with me even through the valley of the shadow of death and yet my heart pounds and I am sick with these feelings which tear at my heart and my very soul. I am not sure that I know who I am anymore and I reach out to You to support me in my distress. Give me the strength and courage to not surrender to my despair and let me feel Your loving presence. You are always with me, even when I cannot feel You. Help me to understand that You will heal me from my distress and restore me to health. Grant me strength to be able not to have to understand these terrible feelings but to trust in You and Your healing even when I feel it not. In my desperation I cry out to You my God and God of all things, hear my prayer ....

"Blessed are You, God, who heals the sick" [20]

---

[19] From the *Amidah* in the Daily Service, *Forms of Prayer* p. 78
[20] idem

Depression

"Out of the depths I call to You,
my living God
God, listen to my voice.
Let Your ears hear the sound
of my pleading" [21]

Source of mercy, help me in this time of need. My soul is full of anguish and my spirit full of disquiet and terror. I see the world as though through a darkened glass. I cannot connect with anyone, not even those I am close to. Even the tender reaching out of friendship and love fills me with a sense of loss and sadness. Why does everything appear so distant from me ? What is the path that lies ahead? Why am I so afraid of what will become of me. Show me Your tenderness, forgiving God. Help me to open myself to Your presence; pour Your spirit into my soul that I may gain the patience for this journey to continue. May I put my trust in You, and understand soon that I, too, am Your creation, formed in Your image and worthy to receive Your love and goodness.

"God is my light and my safety,
whom shall I fear?
God is the strength of my life,
of whom shall I be afraid?" [22]

[21] Psalm 130:1-2
[22] Psalm 27:1

For a good outcome

O Eternal my God, I have taken refuge in You; save me from all that causes me anxiety, and bring a good outcome for me; lest my soul be torn in pieces through my own fear and the trials I am facing; lest my mind be trapped in circling rhythm, so that the darkness of the night and the brightness of the day each bring their own persistent thoughts. Help me to escape from the destruction of my own imaginings, rescue me from monotonous pain.

Let me not be ashamed and confused. Let me not be as chaff before the wind, or walking a dark and slippery way, pursued by I know not what nameless fear or particular dread. Instead let me become aware and fully able, to name my fear and to look upon my dread.

So that my soul shall be joyful in the presence of God; it shall rejoice in my release from the darkness of my pain. All my bones shall say: "God who is like You, who is willing to deliver me from a situation too much for me, to take my unease and apprehension, and to calm and reassure me"[23].

What I now face, God be with me. What I feel may destroy me. Help me to take the measure and respond. I know that the world I experience is not fair, but stay with me in my time of need and help me to journey on, knowing that You are at my side and justice will be found in You. And help me to recognise that I will not ever be truly alone, that whether I know it or not, You will be with me. [24]

---

[23] From the Sabbath service, *Forms of Prayer* p. 203
[24] Based on Psalms 7 and 35

A drug addict

I confess that my life has been an alphabet of woe:
I am an addict;
I have betrayed the trust others had in me;
I have condemned myself to a life of dependency;
I have embittered my loved ones;
I have failed to live up to Your hopes for me;
I have given in to the basest desires that a human could have;
I have hated what I should have loved;
I have injected death into this body which God gave me to cherish;
I have jeered at those who were strong;
I have killed any chance of rehabilitation in others;
I have listened to those whom I should have ignored;
I have mainlined rubbish that I should have rejected;
I have neglected those who loved me;
I have been outrageous in my behaviour;
I have prostituted myself;
I have quarrelled with those who love me;
I have robbed my own family to feed my habit;
I have swallowed drugs which have destroyed my body;
I have taught others to take drugs and undermined their strength;
I have vacillated when I should have been strong;
I have wrecked any resolve I had to give it all away;
I have given way to excess;
I have yielded to the temptation to feel high;
I have had zeal for that life which can only lead to an early death.
Forgive me God. I confess all of this with a sincere heart.

After a failed suicide attempt

Our God and God of our ancestors, You have called us to embrace life, but life is often so bitter for us. We have gone through the storm when life was meaningless and we seriously thought of ending it all. I want to welcome my life. I want to enjoy my life. I know that were I to end my life, those I love would have to live with that pain for ever. Give me the courage to face the day and endure the nights. Give me the perspective to see my storm as temporary: faith to believe that it will soon be over and the energy to see it through. You have given me family and friends whom I love and who love me. Let me grow in strength by enjoying their love.

On lost memories

There are occasions when I am reminded of times and people I had forgotten. Shared times with family and friends, times when my children, now grown, were in my care. In those moments I am given a glimpse of the riches of a good life I was granted, but which I may nonetheless have taken for granted, a life that nourished me, but so much of which has now vanished from memory. If I have lost these treasures due to inattention, to carelessness, or to failure to recognise the great good I have been granted, may I find in my reflections the key to re-opening that store. May my regrets for what has gone and passed from memory spur me to attend more closely to the blessings of my present. May I grow to understand that, though life may be lost to me, it is eternal in You and in the eternal present into which I will one day be gathered

Reflection on growing old

Having passed three score years and ten, even four score years
by reason of strength,
The psalmist and his descendants leave me ill-prepared for
growing old.
Forgetfulness and repetition are a nuisance, but assuaged by
patience and understanding.
Pain and anxiety are constant companions, but love and
attention soothe me.
Inhibitions and embarrassment evaporate in the quest for care.
Experience and achievements are great comforters.
Children - to the third and fourth generations - nurses, doctors,
therapists, all parent me.
Friends and acquaintances disappear with alarming regularity,
through illness, then death.
Will anyone of my generation accompany me on my final
journey?
Yet my curiosity of what lies ahead is still abated, I am in no
rush to join them.
Although I can share David's prayer, "In my old age do not
forsake me"[25],
I more readily empathise with a chasidic interpretation, "Do not
let my world grow old".

---

[25] Psalm 71:18

For achievement

Blessed are You, the Holy One of Blessing, for giving me the courage of my convictions and helping me to achieve this success. I bless You for enabling me to say with pride, "I have done it, I have overcome my fears". I thank You for giving me the fortitude to continue despite obstacles and setbacks.

I bless You for making me what I am, and ask Your blessing upon me that I may continue to achieve in all my endeavours, be they great or small.

3. Special Moments

On your child's first day at school

As you leave home today and enter this new world of yours, go bravely.
Excited in your special grown up clothes, turn your shining face to the fresh experience
Remember that we love you.
Remember that each person you will meet may also be a little bit scared
Remember to ask good questions, and then to listen well to the answers.
It is said that "School children are the flowers on the golden candlestick" [26] of God's sanctuary
Becoming part of the light of understanding, ornamenting the knowledge that will one day be theirs.
So go gently into this world where we cannot follow you,
And begin to become more fully who you are.
Taking first steps into independence, into friendships, into learning
And come back to us at home-time, and teach us of your day.

"May you live to see your world fulfilled; May your destiny be for worlds still to come, and may you trust in generations past and yet to be. May your heart be filled with intuition, and your words filled with insight. May songs of praise ever be upon your tongue, and your vision be in a straight path before you. May your eyes shine with the light of holy words, and your face reflect the brightness of the heavens. May your lips speak wisdom and your fulfilment be in righteousness".[27]

---

[26] Pesikta Rabbati 29b
[27] *Berachot* 17a

On the birth of a grandchild

We give thanks to You, Almighty God, for the opportunity to fulfil Your blessing: "And may you live to see your children's children". [28]

We look forward to helping to raise our new grandchild, to be a support to his/her parents and a source of wise counsel.

We ask for the wisdom to know when to step forward and when to remain silent.

May the other promise of that same psalm be fulfilled for our new grandson/daughter............

May *Adonai* bless you from Zion… all the days of your life.

"Blessed are You, Eternal God, Ruler of the Universe, who has sustained us and kept us and brought us to this season". [29]

---

[28] Psalm 128:6

[29] From *Forms of Prayer* p. 441

On the birth of a non-Jewish grandchild

Eternal God, we give thanks for the birth of our beloved grandchild ………… We pray that s/he may have a life full of health, blessing, peace and joy, surrounded by the love of family and friends.

At this time of celebration, we affirm our special responsibility to be links in the chain of Jewish tradition, so that we can bring the knowledge of our people's relationship with God to the next generation. We do so in humility and love, aware that our treasured grandchild is the offspring of two traditions, and that both must be acknowledge and celebrated.

As we walk this new path, we make a commitment before You, Eternal One our God and God of our ancestors, to do so with sensitivity, humour and care so that we are always aware of the needs of all members of our extended family

We praise You, Eternal God, who gives families reason to celebrate the miracle of life.

Using a *mikveh* when infertile

"This is my beloved and this is my friend
For love is strong as death" [30]

M'kor rachamim[31]- I thank You for the blessing that is contained in my body's abilities and functions, which I should not take for granted. But I also cry out to You in my pain, anxiety and wants. I do not expect an answer, and yet I hope for one.

Help me and my beloved stay strong through the coming month, and remember the strength we share together. We pray that this will be stronger than this monthly remembrance of death, contained within a reminder of the hope for life. Help us not to blame ourselves, or each other, and to accept those blessings we do have, rather than focusing on those we do not.

May I find comfort in the merit of my mothers, Sarah, Rebecca, Rachel and Hannah, who called out to You in their childlessness, and were comforted.

Blessed are You Eternal, who creates each of us whole, and none of us perfect.

---

[30] Song of Songs 5:16, 8:6

[31] "Source of mercy"; the word *rachamim* has its root in *rechem*, meaning womb, and therefore is an appropriate way to address God in this prayer.

On receipt of a decree absolute

God, I stand before You at a time I hoped would never be, when I have to acknowledge the failure of my marriage and the loss of all the hopes with which I entered the state of *kiddushin*, the hope and holiness of Jewish marriage.

Yet, as I look back over my marriage, I see that there were times of hope as well as times of despair, and times of laughter as well as times of tears.

I know that, despite the pain of loss, I would not have been without this experience. I pray for the strength to avoid bitterness, the wisdom to find growth even in the most painful of experiences and the courage to commit again to life with its endless possibilities for love and hope.

Blessed are You, Eternal One, who heals the broken hearted.

On immersion in a *mikveh* after a divorce

As I immerse myself in the waters of life, I call upon the daughters of Israel to be with me as I set myself free. May their strength, determination and faith in the future give me courage, fortitude and hope. May these waters wash away any bitterness or anger within me. Help me to be ready to start a new life.

No longer am I your wife.
No longer are you part of my life.
Now is the time to purify my body and soul.
Now is the time for me to become whole.

With Your guiding hand to lead me, I ask You to heal me of my wounds. With Your love, embrace me. With Your spirit, guide me, now and always.

Lighting the Sabbath candles after losing your partner

Dear God, I pray for the repose of the soul of my dear partner and for the safety and health of my family. I pray that relief and healing will ease the pain and distress of those who have asked for my help this week. Dear God, the synagogues in this town should be a beacon of light spreading Torah to your children; may this be so. I pray for the peace of all the inhabitants of the town and its surroundings and I hope that no word or deed of mine will be a *Chillul Hashem*, a desecration of Your name, but every word and deed of mine to be a *Kiddush Hashem*, a sanctification of Your name.

On kindling a *yahrzeit* candle

I do not need special moments to think of you, for you are always in my thoughts. Nevertheless, I can give thanks for the blessing of your life, your companionship and everything you meant to me. Your absence is still a cause of sadness, but your love lives on, and what we were to each other strengthens and sustains me. You live in my heart and your virtues inspire me to make the most of every day.

Your memory is an abiding blessing

4. Relationships

After a quarrel

"God You search me and know me; You even know my sitting down and my standing up. You understand my thought from afar".[32]

I pray to You, O God, from this most confused place and I entreat Your help in these terrible moments. I feel hurt and angry and confused. I have felt attacked and have attacked back. Hurtful things have been said to me and I have said hurtful things back. I have needed to be right and also I have let my anger run away with me. Sometimes I have not listened to what was said to me. I have wanted to hurt and I have wanted to punish. I have needed to be right more than I have thought about the person I quarrelled with and I have not always been completely true. It is very hard to speak to You because I still feel these terrible feelings in my heart but I struggle to pray now because You are my help and my support in my times of need. Help me to see through all this confusion and listen to myself and listen to the one with whom I have quarrelled. Let that which can be healed, be healed and give us both the strength to be wrong. You know me, O God, for there is not a word on my tongue that You do not know.

"Search me O God and know my heart; try me and know my thoughts: and see if there be any wicked way in me and lead me in the way everlasting".[33]

---

[32] Psalm 139:1-2
[33] Psalm 139:23-24

When feeling betrayed

"It is better to trust in God than it is to trust human beings" [34]

I come to You, O God, because I am hurt and deeply sad. I have trusted and my trust has been betrayed. It seems more than I can bear and it is hard to know where to turn. Let my anger not consume me and let not my desire for some kind of revenge overwhelm me. Protect me from becoming bitter and despising all that is good. It is hard to see that which is good at this time and I can hear myself wanting to turn my back and say that there is nothing good in Your world. I want to hate what I had and say that really none of it was ever good. Help me not to hate and let me put my trust in You. Help me stand up against the bitterness which I know is growing stronger and stronger inside me. Give me the fortitude and courage to try and search for the part I might have played in this betrayal.

"I love God, because God heard my voice and my pleading. Because God listened to me, all my life I will call upon God". [35]

---

[34] Psalm 139:23-24
[35] Psalm 116:1–2

On not being heard

"Hear our voice, our Living God, source of mercy. Spare us and have pity on us, and receive our prayer with love and favour. For You are a God who listens to our prayers and needs". [36]

I speak and yet no one seems to hear what I say. I explain and no one seems to understand. I explain again and again and they do not understand that they do not understand. I am utterly alone and apart from the world. There is no one there, not even You God. I feel that no one cares. I seem to live in a separate and different world and this loneliness is unbearable. It makes me very sad and very angry and I know that in my anger I sometimes hurt those around me. I wish I did not, because then they hate me and blame me and that only makes things worse. Please hear me God, let me know somehow that You are listening. I turn to You with such pain inside me and I have always been taught that You heal all wounds. Let me not be cut off from You and help me with this terrible anger in my heart. Let me feel Your presence once more and be sheltered under the shade of Your Almighty wings. Do not turn me away empty from You for You hear the prayers of all lips.

"Blessed are You God, who listens to prayers". [37]

[36] From the *Amidah* in the Daily Service, *Forms of Prayer* p. 82
[37] idem

For parents when a child leaves home

"To everything there is a season and a time for every purpose under heaven.
A time to embrace and a time to refrain from embracing.
A time to keep hold and a time to let go".[38]

I know that it is never easy to let go. A child grows, becomes more independent and leaves home to begin a new stage in life. This is natural and right, and a moment to celebrate, even if tinged with a sense of loss.

God of Abraham and Sarah, help me as I face the changes this moment brings, and nurture the new relationship that will grow between us.

God of Isaac and Rebecca, may the best of what I have given be fruitful; may the right path lie open ahead.

God of Jacob, Rachel and Leah, be with my child, who is no longer a child, on this journey; guard and guide the life that now begins.

For a boy : Be there for him, as I tried to be there when needed. Guard his going out and his coming in from now on and forever.[39]

For a girl : Be there for her, as I tried to be there when needed. Guard her going out and her coming in from now on and forever.

"May God bless you and keep you.
May God's face shine upon you and be gracious to you.
May God's face turn towards you and give you peace".[40]

---

[38] Ecclesiastes 3:1,5,6
[39] From Psalm 121:8
[40] Numbers 6:24-6

When your parents separate

My parents are not together anymore and I am full of confusion, sadness and anger. The world in which I live is shattered and I do not know who or what I can trust anymore. I feel alone and afraid. I tell myself that I want them back together again but I do not know if that is truly my wish. I want things back the way they were and I know that just cannot be. I tell myself that this is the way things are now and I have to accept it, but I feel that my mother and father have let me down. Could it be my fault even?
Almighty God, I come to You with all these mixed up thoughts and feelings. You command that we love and respect our parents but that is very hard for me to do right now. Give me strength to face what lies before me and help me that my love for my mother and father continues in spite of these other things which invade my mind and my heart. Help my mother and father in what lies before them and be with us all in Your mercy.

"Hear our voice *Adonai* our God. Be gracious and have compassion upon us". [41]

---

[41] From the *Amidah* in the Daily Service, *Forms of Prayer* p. 82

5. Illness and Healing

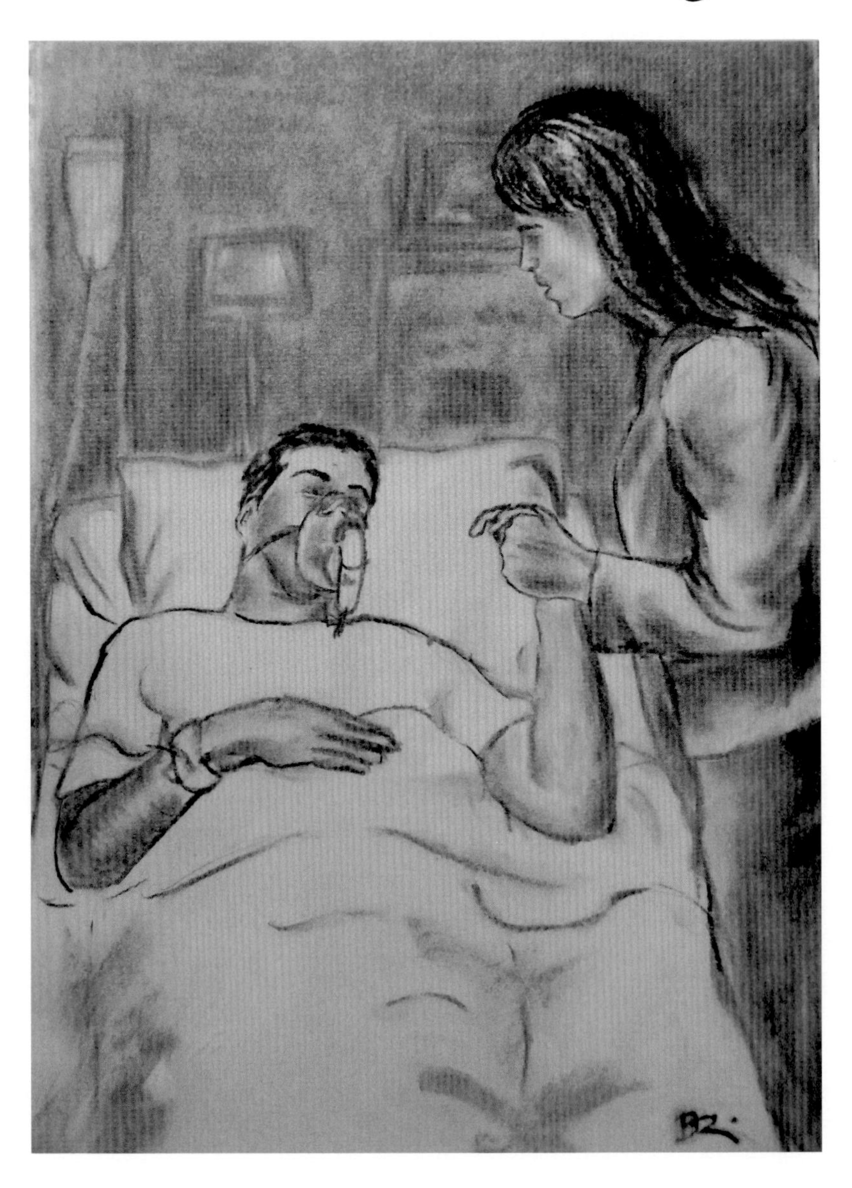

On taking medication

Our God, and God of our ancestors, may it be Your will that my body and my spirit be healed.

For carers

Abraham Ibn Ezra reminds us that there is no one lonelier than the person who loves only themselves. Yet when love becomes responsibility, the strain of the constant task can also be lonely.

******

God strengthen me with patience when caring for this patient.
God strengthen me with the memories of a time when the person
I love so much did not need me in this way.
God strengthen me with the support of others who can help me
when I feel weak.
Blessed are You God, who gives strength to those who care.

Before visiting someone who is sick

I am about to perform the mitzvah of *bikkur cholim* by visiting ......

God, may You join with doctors, nurses and therapists in bringing healing to the sick. May I begin to fulfil my role in this partnership as I dedicate my time, my care and my attention to ..... in their time of need.

Help me to listen to them. Help me to empathise with the pain and anxiety which they feel at this time. Help me to re-assure those others who visit them that they are not alone in their care for .....

"God is my light and my safety, whom shall I fear? God is the strength of my life, of whom shall I be afraid?" [42] As God visited Abraham in his tent as he recovered from pain [43] so may my visit to .... relieve a measure of the pain which ..... feels today.

---

[42] Psalm 27:1
[43] Genesis 18:1

While receiving chemotherapy

I sit here and I wait while the medicine drips into my body. I am afraid, and I am hopeful. May the medicine that has the power to heal or destroy be gentle within me. Give me strength over the next few days, weeks and months to endure the effects of the drugs and illness. While this disease is part of my body, help me to feel powerful and in control of how I live my life. Give me compassion for my doctors, nurses, carers and most of all for my own body. May I know that I am encircled by Your love. May the ancient spirit of the angels Michael, Gabriel, Uriel and Raphael bring me a sense of Your presence, strength, a light at the end of the tunnel, healing and hope.

Before a mastectomy

God, known to us as *El Shaddai*, Source of all power and strength, who enfolds and supports us, in whose image I am made, be with me at this time of terror and desolation which has fallen upon me so suddenly. Remember me and be mindful of me. I am fainting away. My sun has gone down while it is still day, I am confused and confounded [44]. My heart moans within me, my eyes are a fountain of tears. Help me to see that my world still exists, my life is still to be lived, my self is not destroyed.

Now that I must begin a journey of damage and destruction, of pain and grief;

- help me to keep faith with those who seek to cure me,
- help me to trust the healing that is brought about by such an injury,
- teach me to hold fast to the person I am and let go of the fear and loneliness which threaten to overwhelm me.

Be with me *El Shaddai*, You who know the meaning of my life,

- give me strength and courage, trust and hope,
- cover me in the shelter of Your wings
- hold me to Your breasts and comfort me.

Deliver me from illness, I run to Your sheltering presence, for You are my God, Your spirit is good.

For Your own name, God, cause me to live most fully,
For Your own righteousness bring my soul out from this trouble.
And in Your great mercy cut me away from my adversaries,
destroy all who afflict my soul, for I am Your servant [45]

[44] adapted from Jeremiah 15:9
[45] adapted from Psalm 143:9-12

Whilst waiting for someone undergoing a medical procedure

As I pass the one I love into the care of medical professionals, I turn to God with hope and fear. I ask God to give these doctors the wisdom to perform this task and the compassion to treat their patients with concern and respect. I ask God to give my
.... the strength to make a *refuah shlemah* – a complete healing of both body and mind. My task is only to wait, but I ask God to give me the peace of mind to wait not in fear but in the knowledge that the God of Israel neither slumbers nor sleeps but shelters me in the shadow of God's wings and supports me in times of trial.

Blessed are You God, our guide and guardian.

For the partner of someone undergoing surgery or chemotherapy

Adonai, I stand before You this day full of such strong emotion that I am almost unable to speak. I pray for strength to be there for the one I love so deeply, to support him/her in this time of trouble and distress. I pray for the depth of understanding that comes from You, that will allow me to hear his/her fear, and be aware of his/her concerns at this life-changing event. I know that healing comes from You, Eternal One, and I pray that my beloved will come through this time of trial with as little pain as possible, able to bless once again this opportunity for renewed life

But God, I must also give voice to my fear, that terrible concern that the medical intervention may not be successful. Thank you for the chance to voice my inner worries to You, who are closer to me than my very heartbeat. Knowing that You are there, holding me gently under the wings of the *Shechinah*, allows me to be strong for the one I love

Blessed are You, Eternal One, who supports the fallen and raises up those who are bowed down.

For healing if possible

Our God, God of the generations, our God, God of all.

God, Eternal One, God of Sarah, Rebeccah, Leah and Rachel.
God of Abraham and Isaac and Jacob, of Israel.
God the near one, the far one, the dear one, the dark one.
God of our sorrows and God of our joys.
God of our illnesses and God of our healing.

What can we ask, but to cry and stammer and pour out our hearts to You.

Turn Your face of mercy towards him, and grant him
  healing in his body, healing in his very being.
May the One who heals
Give him back to his parents, his family,
His friends, and the city of which he is so vital a part.

And, *Adonai*, Eternal One,
Give strength and courage to his mother on his left,
And his father on his right.
Angels of holiness,
Messengers of Your love.

God, please heal him.

6. Birth and Death

After the moment of birth

My child, I have known you for many months.
I have felt the first stirrings of your limbs form and harden against my belly.
I have seen your faint form on the hospital scanner.
But only now do I see you in your wondrous wholeness, your wondrous
smallness, your wondrous perfection.
I hear your cry, I feel your smoothness, I smell your newness and give
thanks.

"Eternal our God, how magnificent is Your name throughout the earth.
Your splendour is counted over the heavens.
From the mouths of babies and sucklings You have established strength...
When I see Your heavens and the work of Your fingers,
the moon and stars that You established,
what is humanity that You remember it?
and the children of human beings that You take notice?
and that You have made them little less than angels?
and have crowned them with glory and honour?" [46]

"And God created humanity in the divine image. In the image of
God was humanity created. Male and female God created them". [47]
"Thus says the Eternal, your redeemer, who formed you from the womb, I
the Eternal make all things". [48]

[46] Psalm 8:1-6
[47] Genesis 1:27
[48] Isaiah 44:24

A mother's prayer on the circumcision of her son

God and God of our ancestors, You gave me this gift of a child
in all his beauty.
Now You require a part of him in rejection of ancient cruelties -
a part for the whole.
Now You require blood from him - his second birth into
himself.
Help me to see this not as mutilation but as perfection;
humanities' contribution to the partnership of creation;
working with God in *tikkun olam*.[49]
Help me to see this not as his removal from my sphere of gentle
creativity into a male world of brutality; but as his entry into
our rich inheritance; his bonding with and binding to the faith
of our forebears.

If other women are present they say:

Just as he enters into the covenant, so may he also enter into the blessings of Torah, of marriage and of good deeds.

The mother responds:

Blessed are You, our Living God, who remembers the covenant.

---

[49] Perfection of the world

After a miscarriage

Eternal our God,
For a time You gave us the hope of a new life,
Placed in us the expectation of a new awakening.
Now in Your wisdom,
You have taken that hope from us,
have delayed, for reasons only known to You,
the arrival of that new soul into our world.

God, we thank You still for the hope You gave us,
And pray that You may renew in us that hope in time to come;
though the pain of our disappointment is real and deep
we acknowledge still that You are our God,
You renew life beyond death.
You give, and take away,
You hold all our souls in the palm of Your hand.

May it be Your will to give us, once more,
the chance to share with You
in the bringing of new life to this our world;
May it be Your will that we shall be strengthened,
both by our hopes
and our disappointments,
and learn to love the more deeply, that which we have.
Blessed are You, God, who shares the sorrow of Your creation.

After the termination of a pregnancy

Be gracious to me, God, for I am in distress; my eye is consumed with grief, my soul and my body. My life is spent with grief, my strength fails, I am like a broken vessel. Let me not be ashamed, Eternal, for I have called on You. I said in my haste, "I am cut off from before Your eyes", but still You heard the voice of my entreaties when I cried to You. There are those who say that God has forsaken me. God, do not be far from me and make haste to help me. Restore me back to life, bring me back from the depths of the earth. You are my hope. You have searched me and known me, You are acquainted with all my ways. Out of the depths I cry to You, my God, hear my voice. How long shall I take counsel in my soul, having sorrow in my heart daily ? How long will You hide Your face from me? As for me I will behold Your face in righteousness. I will be satisfied when I awake, beholding Your likeness. [50]

[50] The following psalms are used to create this prayer : 31, 71, 139, 130, 13, 17.

At the bedside of a dying person

I sit with you now and do not know if you can hear me.
I watch your breathing and wonder when the last breath will come.
When will you really be gone? What of you is left here with me?
I sit and I remember who you were, who I was with you;
Now we are both someone else and the link between us is altered.
Do you know I am here? And does it bring you comfort?
Do you want me to leave, am I holding you tethered to this place?
I want to ask you and yet I am so frightened.
Do you want to leave? Am I in your way?
I would ask God for your release. I would ask God for my release
But I do not know what it is I really want to be released into.
Or where you would go.
But I sit with you now and do not know if you can feel me
Loving you, and crying, letting go.

On the death of a pet

O God, I mourn the passing of my beloved ......who has entered the life of everlasting peace. I give thanks for the years of loyalty and companionship that we have enjoyed, and all the memories of happiness which we have shared. I shall always cherish memories of the time we spent together. My beloved .....will continue to live in my heart.

7. Facing the World

Before turning the key in the car ignition for the first time that day

Please God, may I remember that I am driving a potentially lethal instrument. May I not harm any one or any thing. May no person or thing harm me. If I can be helpful today, may I please be so. And may I return safely to my home at the end of the day.

When getting on an aeroplane

"You were borne on eagle's wings"[51]. A short time from now I will be flying high in the air. I will be supported by the same forces which You created for the birds of the air so that they could fly with as much ease as a person can walk. The pilot and his or her assistants will use their skills to ensure that I am safe in this world so different from the stability of the ground.

We will travel together to traverse the world at speeds impossible by any other method. We will soar above the clouds and see the world from a perspective closer to Yours. The dividing lines of borders, nationality and language will disappear for these hours as what I can see below me becomes one world and one humanity living in it, dominated by sea, mountains and forest. I will entrust myself to Your care and that of those endowed with the skills to use the forces of flight to transport me, traversing rough and smooth air with the competence that the birds share unconcerned.

"The earth and its fullness belong to God, the world and those who dwell in it" [52]. As we cross the Earth in Your higher realm, lead us to our destination in safety.

---

[51] Deuteronomy 32:11
[52] Psalm 24:1

Before a committee meeting

Let us come together in God's name and prepare ourselves to do God's will.

May Your presence dwell among us, drawing us to serve You and Your creatures with justice and with love. Let us listen to each other with respect, and treat each other with wisdom and generosity, so that we witness to the Creator we serve, and justify Your choice of us.

May none of our controversies rise up like those of Korach, from ambition and self-seeking. Let them only be for the sake of heaven, like those of Hillel and Shammai. May our eyes be open to see Your greatness in the smallest things we do.

Through our faithfulness may the cause of goodness prosper in the world.

May the favour of the Creator, our God, be upon us to support us in the work we do.

"May God support the work we do".[53]

---

[53] Psalm 90:17

Before an inter-faith meeting

God of all creation, we stand in awe before You, impelled by the visions of human harmony. We are children of many traditions - inheritors of shared wisdom and tragic misunderstandings, of proud hopes and humble successes. Now it is time for us to meet - in memory and truth, in courage and trust, in love and promise.

In that which we share, let us see the common prayer of humanity; where we differ, let us wonder at human freedom; in our unity and our differences, let us know the uniqueness that is God.

May our courage match our convictions, and our integrity match our hope.

May our faith in You bring us closer to each other.

May our meeting with past and present bring blessing for the future.

On seeing a fire engine or ambulance on its way to an emergency

Please God, if it be Your will, may the crews arrive on time to save those hurt or trapped, and grant strength to all those involved in this emergency.

After a natural disaster

Eternal One, our Rock and our Refuge, You are the source of our trust and our salvation. To You we turn with thoughts and prayers for those whose lives were lost.

We think of those who died, of those who lost all that was precious and dear to them, family, friends, homes and possessions, of those whose lives are now blighted with loss, suffering, disease and poverty and who cry out to You: "Save me, O God; I am weary with my crying; my throat is parched, my eyes grow dim". [54]

O God, do not be far from those who cry out to You; guide us in all that we undertake on their behalf. As You support the needy when they call, may we respond with generosity and compassion; as You have pity on the weak and poor, so may we help save the lives of those in danger, alleviate their suffering and bring hope and help to those who have survived and must rebuild their lives.

You are our God; in You shall be our faithfulness and steadfast love, for You are our God and the rock of our salvation.

"So long as the earth endures,
seedtime and harvest, cold and heat,
summer and winter, day and night,
shall not cease". [55]

---

[54] Psalm 69:2, 4
[55] Genesis 8:22

Upon war

At this time of conflict we turn to You, God, as the Creator of all human beings, each of us made in Your image, each of us equal in Your sight. Our sages have taught, "whoever takes a single human life, it is as if they have destroyed an entire world". [56]

They also taught, "in that hour in which the Egyptians drowned in the Sea of Reeds, the angels wished to sing a song of praise before God. But God rebuked them saying, 'My children are drowning in the sea, would you utter a song before Me in honour of that ?' " [57]

Be with Your children of all nations and religions, and give them strength and courage in this time of uncertainty and fear. Any war claims its victims on all sides. Have mercy on them and bring this conflict speedily to an end, so that its casualties may be few and damage be light; so that acts of violence and bloodshed maybe replaced with words and acts of conciliation. Shelter under Your care those who perish and show compassion to those who mourn for them. For those injured in body or mind, bring a perfect healing, so that their lives are not destroyed.

May the One who brings
peace in the highest,
bring peace to us and to all Israel
and to the whole world
and let us say, Amen.

---

[56] *Avot d'Rabbi Natan 31*
[57] *Megillah* 10b

On the anniversary of the London bombings

Sometimes we number and sometimes we name.
There are those we have lost, and we remember.
We remember their lives and we remember their names.
And there are those that we ourselves never knew.
Though each had a name, we remember them in number.
While others will remember them in name.
7/7 when
52 were murdered by explosion.
52 they were in number;
7/7 the day's number is its name.
God saw how great human wickedness can be.
Who will stand up for me against those who do evil and act wickedly?
Were God not my support, my soul would be dumfounded.
When I think I might stumble,
O God, may Your lovingkindness support me.
When I am filled with confusion,
may Your assurance soothe my soul.
They band together to do away with the righteous;
they condemn the innocent to death.
But the Almighty is my refuge;
my God is my sheltering rock.

In silence, we remember those whose lives were cut short in the indiscriminate violence of the 7/7 bombings.[58]

---

[58] with references to Genesis 6:5; Psalm 94:16-19; 21-22

Composition of the Prayers

Prayers that first appeared elsewhere are marked with an asterisk

1. Situations that test us

Before an exam - Howard Cooper

Before an exam, for a parent - Sylvia Rothschild

Before a driving test - Sylvia Rothschild

Before a major sporting event - Howard Cooper

On making an investment - Mark Goldsmith

On losing a job - Mark Goldsmith

During unemployment - Howard Cooper

Upon bankruptcy - David Freeman

On retirement* - Jonathan Magonet

2. Confronting ourselves

An insomniac's prayer - Howard Cooper

Anxiety - David Freeman

Depression* - Alexandra Wright

For a good outcome - Sylvia Rothschild

A drug addict - Brian Fox

After a failed suicide attempt - Brian Fox

On lost memories - Tony Hammond

Reflection on growing old - Maurice Michaels

For achievement - Marcia Plumb (adapted from a blessing written by Patricia Tausz)

3. Special moments

4. Relationships

5. Illness and healing

6. Birth and death

7. Facing the World

Before turning the key in the car ignition for the first time that day - Jackie Tabick

When getting on an aeroplane - Mark Goldsmith

Before a committee meeting* - Lionel Blue and Jonathan Magonet

Before an inter-faith meeting* - Jonathan Magonet

On seeing a fire engine or ambulance on its way to an emergency - Jackie Tabick

After a natural disaster* - Alexandra Wright

Upon war* - Sylvia Rothschild

On the anniversary of the London Bombings - Paul Freedman

* taken from *Forms of Prayer*, London : The Movement for Reform Judaism, 2008

** taken from *Taking Up the Timbrel*, eds : Sylvia Rothschild and Sybil Sheridan, London : SCM Press, 2000

*** taken from *Faith and Practice : A Guide to Reform Judaism Today*, Jonathan Romain, London : The Movement for Reform Judaism, 1991

**** taken from *Seder Tefillot B'vet Evel*, London : Liberal Judaism, 1996

Biographical Notes

MIRIAM BERGER (b.1979) studied Theology at the University of Bristol and was ordained by the Leo Baeck College in 2006. She is the Principal Rabbi of Finchley Reform Synagogue and is the daughter of Rabbi Tony Bayfield and the late Linda Bayfield.

LIONEL BLUE was one of the first two ordinees of the Leo Baeck College in 1958. He assisted small Progressive communities in Europe before serving as the minister to the Settlement Synagogue and then Middlesex New Synagogue. He became Convener of the Reform *Beth Din*, while he achieved national fame for his religious broadcasts on radio and television. He has written numerous books and in 1993 received the Templeton Prize.

BARBARA BORTS was ordained in 1981 by Leo Baeck College. She was rabbi at Radlett and Bushey Reform Synagogue, and involved in social issues. She returned to North America, working in congregations, as a chaplain, and in Montreal as an adult Jewish studies educator. She is now rabbi of Newcastle Reform Synagogue, of a small group in Switzerland, is pursuing a PhD at University of Durham University and studying *chazzanut.*

HOWARD COOPER is a psychoanalytic psychotherapist, lecturer and writer. He is the author of *The Alphabet of Paradise: An A-Z of Spirituality for Everyday Life* and blogs on themes of Jewish interest at howardcoopersblog.blogspot.com

BRIAN FOX has been Rabbi at Menorah Synagogue in Manchester since 1999. He served congregations in Melbourne ('72-'79) and Sydney ('79-'99). A founder of Jewish Day Schools in both those cities, he is a passionate Zionist and continues to work for the cause of Israel. He received the Order of Australia (AM) for his interfaith work. Married to Dale and they have 4 children and 3 grandchildren.

PAUL FREEDMAN studied Physics at Bristol, Education at Cambridge and for the rabbinate at Leo Baeck College, where he has lectured in Biblical Hebrew. Previously he was Head of Science of a large secondary school in Gloucestershire. He is on the Editorial Board of the Reform *siddur*, Vice-Chair of the Assembly of Reform Rabbis, Rabbi of Radlett & Bushey Reform Synagogue, married to Vanessa and father of Katie and Joshua.

DAVID FREEMAN was ordained at the Leo Baeck College in 1967, was a congregational rabbi for 21 years during which time he also served as University and Hospice Chaplain. He is also a professional member and ex Chair of The Association of Jungian Analysts, a supervisor, training analyst and external examiner in various psychotherapy trainings. He is a past Chair of The Guild of Pastoral Psychology and lectures in Europe.

HELEN FREEMAN was born in Surrey and qualified as a speech therapist. After rabbinic ordination in 1990 she served the Liberal Jewish Synagogue and is now at West London Synagogue. She wrote articles on *Chochmah* and Healing and on a Ritual to Follow Divorce in the two books published by the women rabbis of the United Kingdom. She followed up her interest in healing by training as a Jungian analyst.

MARK GOLDSMITH is Principal Rabbi of North Western Reform Synagogue (Alyth). He gained *semichah* in 1996 and has since served both Liberal and Reform congregations in London. His main study interest is the intersection between Judaism and working life, particularly in the area of investment. He has been Chairperson of the Rabbinic Conference of Liberal Judaism. He and his wife, Nicola, have two daughters.

TONY HAMMOND is rabbi at Bromley Reform Synagogue since 2004. Previously taught English and French Literature in schools and universities, then director and lecturer in Jewish History and modern Jewish Literature at LJCC (formerly Spiro Institute).

SIDNEY KAY, born Manchester 1920, trained as a mechanical engineer, served in army in Normandy, Belgium, Holland and Germany, and was present at the liberation of Belsen Concentration Camp. He was married to his late wife Lily for 62 years. He served both Reform and Liberal congregations and is now Rabbi Emeritus of Southport Reform Synagogue.

JOSH LEVY was ordained at Leo Baeck College, 2007. He is a member of the rabbinic team at Alyth – North Western Reform Synagogue.

JONATHAN MAGONET was Principal of Leo Baeck College for twenty years till his retirement in 2005. He continues as Emeritus Professor of Bible. He has pioneered Jewish-Christian and Jewish-Christian-Muslim dialogue, edits the journal *European Judaism* and is the editor of the new 8th edition of *Seder Ha-t'fillot, Forms of Prayer*. His books include *A Rabbi Reads the Bible* and *A Rabbi Reads the Psalms*.

MAURICE MICHAELS came to the rabbinate later in life following a successful career in industry. As student and since *s'michah* he has served Harlow Jewish Community, EDRS and SWESRS. His major interests have been in Education and Interfaith, in which he has made his main contribution to the local community. He teaches Practical Rabbinics at Leo Baeck College and dedicates his prayers in this book to his recently deceased father.

CHARLES MIDDLEBURGH is Honorary Director of Studies at Leo Baeck College; Rabbi, Cardiff Reform Synagogue and Dublin Jewish Progressive Congregation; Fellow, Zoological Society of London.

MARCIA PLUMB is one of the rabbis at Southgate and District Reform Synagogue, the Rabbi on staff for Akiva School, and the Director of the Spiritual Formation Programme at Leo Baeck College, London. She is trained in Jewish Spiritual Counselling and does one to one spiritual counselling as well as in groups. She was born in Houston Texas, and is a contributor to several books and journals.

JONATHAN ROMAIN is rabbi of Maidenhead Synagogue. He writes regularly for *The Times*, *Guardian* and *Jewish Chronicle* and appears on radio and television. His nine books include *The Jews of England* and *Faith and Practice : A Guide to Reform Judaism Today*. He received the MBE for his work with mixed-faith couples nationally. He is also chaplain to the Jewish Police Association.

SYLVIA ROTHSCHILD grew up in Bradford. Ordained in 1987 she served Bromley Synagogue for 15 years and is now pioneering a new model of working in the rabbinate, job sharing the role with Sybil Sheridan in Wimbledon. Her interest in writing new prayers was given impetus when in her first week as rabbi she found there was no funeral service for a stillborn child. She has written ever since.

WALTER ROTHSCHILD, born Bradford 1954; served Sinai Synagogue (plus Bradford, Hull, Sheffield communities) 1984-1994, then communities in Vienna, Aruba, Berlin, München, Schleswig-Holstein, Köln, Halle, Freiburg. PhD (King's College London) on 'Palestine Railways 1945-1948'. Publisher of *Harakevet*, magazine on Middle East Railways. Published: *Tales of the Chutzper Rebbe* (Alef, California); *Auf das Leben!* (Goldmann, München); *99 Fragen zum Judentum* and *Der Honig und der Stachel* (Gütersloher). Innumerable articles, poems, translations, *Songs My Dybbuk Taught Me.*

SYBIL SHERIDAN read Theology and Religious Studies at Cambridge University and was ordained by the Leo Baeck College in 1981. She served as rabbi to the Ealing Liberal Synagogue, the Thames Valley Progressive Jewish Community and is currently at the Wimbledon and District Synagogue (Reform). A former lecturer at the Leo Baeck College and the Muslim College, she wrote *Stories from the Jewish World*, edited *Hear Our Voice*, co-edited *Taking up the Timbrel.*

JACKIE TABICK is rabbi of North West Surrey Synagogue , Weybridge. Married to Larry, Reform rabbi in Hampstead and mother of three grown children. Jackie gained *s'michah* from Leo Baeck College in 1975 and has worked in communities continuously from that date. She is also interested in interfaith and social justice work, is a patron of JCore, on the executive of the Interfaith Network and chairs the World Congress of Faiths.

ALEXANDRA WRIGHT studied for the rabbinate at Leo Baeck College and was ordained in 1986. She served as Associate Rabbi at the Liberal Jewish Synagogue before moving to Radlett & Bushey Reform Synagogue in 1990. She returned to the LJS in 2004 as Senior Rabbi, the first woman to hold a senior post in the UK.

DEBBIE YOUNG-SOMERS was ordained from Leo Baeck College in the summer of 2009. She has previously worked in interfaith and educational roles, and has enjoyed being with several communities whilst studying. She has a particular interest in developing a Progressive use of the *mikveh* and creative rituals in general.

Other publications available from the Movement for Reform Judaism

FORMS OF PRAYER

Daily and Sabbath Siddur

Pilgrim Festivals Machzor
(Pesach, Shavuot Sukkot, Simchat Torah)

High Holydays Machzor
(Days of Awe : Rosh Hashanah and Yom Kippur)

BOOKS

Faith and Practice - A Guide to Reform Judaism Today
by Rabbi Dr Jonathan Romain

God, Doubt and Dawkins - Reform Rabbis respond to The God Delusion
edited by Rabbi Dr Jonathan Romain

To Heaven with Scribes & Pharisees
by Rabbi Lionel Blue

Tradition and Change - A History of Reform Judaism in Britain 1840-1995
by Anne J Kershen and Rabbi Dr Jonathan Romain

Werner van der Zyl - Master Builder
A Collection of Essays about his Life and Work

'RESPONSA' SERIES

Bar Mitzvah and Bat Mitzvah - A Reform Perspective

by Rabbi Dr. Michael Hilton

D-I-Y Rituals - A Guide To Creating Your Own Jewish Rituals

by Rabbi Laura Janner-Klausner

I'm Jewish, My Partner Isn't

by Rabbi Dr. Jonathan Romain

Kashrut for Pesach

by Rabbi Dr. Michael Hilton

Marriage

by Rabbi Rachel Montagu

Mixed Faith Burials

by Rabbi Dr. Jonathan Romain

PAMPHLET

What is Reform Judaism?

by Rabbi Tony Bayfield

For orders details, contact the Movement for Reform Judaism,

The Sternberg Centre, 80 East End Road, London N3 2SY

0208-349-4731 www.reformjudaism.org.uk